IGBO

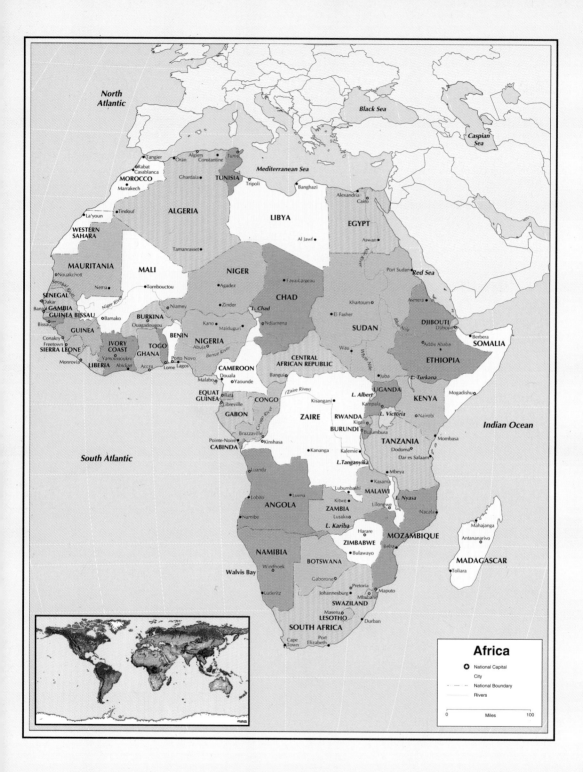

North
Atlantic

Black Sea

Caspian
Sea

Tangier
Rabat
Casablanca
MOROCCO
Marrakech

Algiers
Oran
Constantine
Tunis
TUNISIA

Ghardaia

Tripoli

Mediterranean Sea

Banghazi

Alexandria
Cairo

La'youn
Tindouf

ALGERIA

LIBYA

EGYPT

WESTERN
SAHARA

Tamanrasset

Al Jawf

Aswan

MAURITANIA

MALI

NIGER

Nile River

Port Sudan
Red Sea

Nouakchott

Nema

Tombouctou

Agadez

Faya-Largeau

CHAD

Khartoum

Asmera

SENEGAL
Dakar
Banjul GAMBIA
GUINEA BISSAU
Bissau
GUINEA
Conakry
Freetown
SIERRA LEONE
Monrovia
LIBERIA

Senegal River
Niger River
Bamako
Niger River
Niamey
BURKINA
Ouagadougou

Zinder
L. Chad
Kano
Maiduguri
Ndjamena

El Fasher

SUDAN

Blue Nile

DJIBOUTI
Djibouti
Berbera
SOMALIA

Addis Ababa
ETHIOPIA

BENIN
NIGERIA
Abuja
Benue River

IVORY
COAST
Yamoussoukro
GHANA
TOGO
Porto Novo
Lome Lagos
Accra

Wau

White Nile

L. Turkana

Abidjan

CAMEROON
Douala
Yaounde
Bangui

CENTRAL
AFRICAN REPUBLIC

Mogadishu

EQUAT
GUINEA
Bata
Libreville
GABON

Malabo

CONGO

(Zaire River)

Kisangani

L. Albert
UGANDA
Kampala

Juba

KENYA

Nairobi

Congo River

ZAIRE

RWANDA
Kigali
BURUNDI
Bujumbura

L. Victoria

Mombasa

Indian Ocean

Brazzaville
Pointe-Noire
Kinshasa
CABINDA

Kananga

Kalemie

TANZANIA
Dodoma
Dar es Salaam

South Atlantic

Luanda

L. Tanganyika

Mbeya

Kasama

Lobito
Luena

Lubumbashi
Kitwe
MALAWI
L. Nyasa

Nacala

Namibe
ANGOLA

ZAMBIA
Lusaka

Lilongwe

Mahajanga

Antananarivo

L. Kariba
Harare
ZIMBABWE
Bulawayo

MOZAMBIQUE
Beira

MADAGASCAR
Toliara

NAMIBIA
Windhoek

BOTSWANA

Walvis Bay

Gaborone

Luderitz

Johannesburg

Pretoria
Maputo
Mbabane
SWAZILAND
Maseru
LESOTHO
Durban

SOUTH AFRICA

Cape
Town
Port
Elizabeth

Africa

✪ National Capital
○ City
National Boundary
Rivers

0   Miles   100

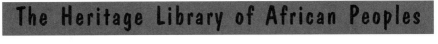

The Heritage Library of African Peoples

IGBO

Kalu Ogbaa, Ph.D.

THE ROSEN PUBLISHING GROUP, INC.
NEW YORK

To All My Children
Ikenna, Ndubuisi, Emeka, Nneka, Enyinna, and Kelechi,
and other Igbo children abroad, who must be reminded
always of their noble heritage.

Published in 1995 by The Rosen Publishing Group, Inc.
29 East 21st Street, New York, NY 10010

First Edition

Library of Congress Cataloging-in-Publication Data

Ogbaa, Kalu.
    Igbo / Kalu Ogbaa.
       p.   cm. — (The heritage library of African peoples)
    Includes bibliographical references and index.
    ISBN 0-8239-1977-3
    1. Igbo (African people)—Juvenile literature. I. Title.
  II. Series.
  DT515. 45. I330325 1995
  966. 9' 4400496332—dc20
                                94-36608
                                    CIP
                                    AC

Contents

INTRODUCTION

THERE IS EVERY REASON FOR US TO KNOW something about Africa and to understand its past and the way of life of its peoples. Africa is a rich continent that has for centuries provided the world with art, culture, labor, wealth, and natural resources. It has vast mineral deposits, fossil fuels, and commercial crops.

But perhaps most important is the fact that fossil evidence indicates that human beings originated in Africa. The earliest traces of human beings and their tools are almost two million years old. Their descendants have migrated throughout the world. To be human is to be of African descent.

The experiences of the peoples who stayed in Africa are as rich and as diverse as of those who established themselves elsewhere. This series of books describes their environment, their modes of subsistence, their relationships, and their customs and beliefs. The books present the variety of languages, histories, cultures, and religions that are to be found on the African continent. They demonstrate the historical linkages between African peoples and the way contemporary Africa has been affected by European colonial rule.

Africa is large, complex, and diverse. It encompasses an area of more than 11,700,000

square miles. The United States, Europe, and India could fit easily into it. The sheer size is an indication of the continent's great variety in geography, terrain, climate, flora, fauna, peoples, languages, and cultures.

Much of contemporary Africa has been shaped by European colonial rule, industrialization, urbanization, and the demands of a world economic system. For more than seventy years, large regions of Africa were ruled by Great Britain, France, Belgium, Portugal, and Spain. African peoples from various ethnic, linguistic, and cultural backgrounds were brought together to form colonial states.

For decades Africans struggled to gain their independence. It was not until after World War II that the colonial territories become independent African states. Today, almost all of Africa is ruled by Africans. Large numbers of Africans live in modern cities. Rural Africa is also being transformed, and yet its people still engage in many of their age-old customs and beliefs.

Contemporary circumstances and natural events have not always been kind to ordinary Africans. Today, however, new popular social movements and technological innovations pose great promise for future development.

George C. Bond, Ph.D., Director
Institute of African Studies
Columbia University, New York

The Igbo have longstanding and respected traditions. With her face and body painted with indigo *uli* patterns, this young girl takes part in an annual festival.

chapter

1

THE IGBO

THE IGBO (PRONOUNCED IBO) ARE A DISTIN-
guished group of people who live in southeastern
Nigeria. In numbers alone, the Igbo are one of
the three dominent ethnic groups of Nigeria, with
the Hausa and the Yoruba. The other two groups
are found in other parts of Africa. The Igbo are
found only in Nigeria. Their achievements have
been significant in such fields as art, agriculture,
politics, economics, and, above all, education,
both in Nigeria and on the African continent.

The language of the Igbo is also called Igbo. It
is a member of the Kwa language subfamily of
West Africa, which was developed as a separate
language about 4,500 years ago. However, the
language remained unwritten until the late 19th
century, when the British colonists established
mission schools and churches (following their

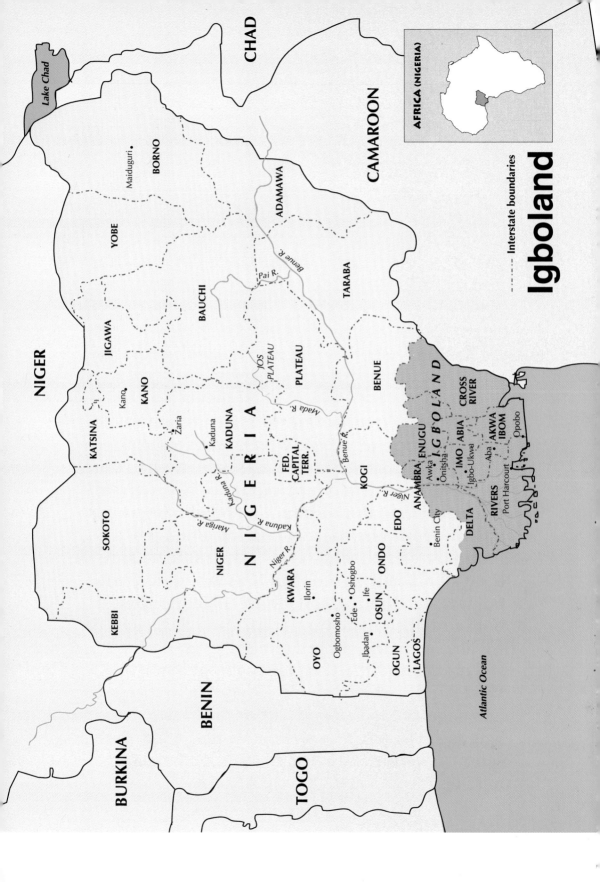

colonization of Igboland). The missionaries developed the Igbo orthography that enabled them to translate the Bible into Igbo.

Until recently, what was known of Igbo origins came from Igbo folktales and oral history. Some of the elders maintained that, "We did not come from anywhere, and anyone who tells you that we came from anywhere is a liar." In fact, the Igbo believe that their creator, Chukwu, put them in Igboland the minute the world was created, and that they did not migrate from any other part of the world. That, perhaps, explains why there are no other Igbo-speaking peoples elsewhere in the world.

From the early nucleus of settlement in northern Igboland, the Igbo people have spread south and west. Today, they inhabit exclusively the Abia, Anambra, Enugu, and Imo states of Nigeria; but they are found also in large numbers in Akwa Ibom, Delta, Lagos, and Rivers states. All in all, the Igbo number about 13.5 million, according to the 1991 Nigerian Census.▲

chapter

2

IGBOLAND

THE ORGANIZATION OF TRADITIONAL IGBO society begins at the village level. The village (*ama, obodo,* or *mba* in Igbo) is a community of people who are descendants of one or more male ancestors. These ancestors are usually the founders of the village.

The village begins as a nuclear family of one man and one or more wives, who live in the same household, the *obi*. As the male children grow and multiply, they build their own separate households in the same area. These families, *umunna*, in turn, multiply and become a bloc, *ezi*. A number of blocs grow into a village, and villages into clans, many of which combine to form Igboland, *ndi Igbo*.

▼ THE IGBO FAMILY ▼
The Igbo family consists of a man, one or

Several small villages are nestled in this northern Igbo savanna.

more wives, and their children. The marriage institution is patrilocal, which means that a married couple must live in the husband's home or compound. If there is divorce, the woman is the one to leave the house and return to her parents' home or her birthplace. Also, family succession is patriarchal, meaning that the father is the head of the family, and descent is traced through the male line.

▼ IGBO WORLDVIEW ▼
In spite of their society's being patriarchal, the Igbo believe in complementary dualism.

13

That is the belief that opposite beings, including humans, complement each other in order to become whole and effective. That is why the Igbo talk of *elu na ala* (the sky and the earth), *nwoke na nwanyi* (man and woman), and *udu miri na okochi* (wet and dry seasons). The sky or the heavenly dome is firmly in place because the earth gives it support; and the earth is able to yield crops because the sky gives it rain. In the same manner, a woman can give birth to a child because she is made pregnant by a man; and the man cannot have children unless the woman is able and willing to bear them.

The Igbo view of their world is that Igboland is both a physical and metaphysical (outside of the physical) reality. It consists of the "three worlds"—living ancestors beneath the earth (*ala mmo*); the living people on earth (*elu uwa*); and babies in the womb (*akpa nnwa*).

▼ ALA, THE EARTH GODDESS ▼

What affects beings in one of the "worlds" affects others in the other "worlds." And life in all three "worlds" is regulated by the pan-Igbo goddess of the earth, Ala. Ala is in charge of human morality and fertility. Hence, any crime or immoral or unethical act that people commit is a crime against Ala, *nso Ala,* as well as a crime against (the laws of the) land. On the other hand, moral and ethical behaviors derive

Kola nuts are shared ceremonially at all social gatherings, when prayers
are directed to "spirit beings," Igbo ancestors.

from *omenala*, custom (that is, sanctioned by the
goddess) of the land.

The Igbo do not separate religious morality
from political morality, and every place is re-
garded as "holy ground" since it is part of the
earth, which embodies Ala.

▼ RELIGIOUS VERSUS SECULAR LIFE ▼

As a result of the Igbo's worldview, their
religious life influences their secular life very
much. They pour libations of wine, break kola
nut, and say incantations to invite the ancestors
and the unborn babies—"spirit beings"—to their
meals and meetings.

These *ekwe* masks of several carved wooden figures are dramatic to see, but difficult to dance in because of their weight.

Because of the presence of such spirit beings, every living person is careful about what he or she does or says. At the end of the meeting, the decision that the people make is binding on everybody.

The spirit beings are represented by masquerades, *mmanwu,*who appear during ceremonies and festivals. Public ceremonies, such as the New Yam Festival and Naming of Age-grades, create opportunities for interaction between human beings and ancestors seasonally and annually. They serve as effective forms of social control.▲

A Compound Chief heads each Igbo village.

chapter

3

SOCIAL STRUCTURE

THE SOCIAL STRUCTURE OF IGBOLAND IS
somewhat complicated. However, at the base of
that structure is the village.

▼ STRUCTURES OF GOVERNANCE ▼

Each village is made up of compounds, whose
heads are the oldest men (with their wives)
known as Compound Chiefs, *Ndi Eze Ezi*.
Together the group of Compound Chiefs form
the Village Council, *Ndi Ichie*. Their social and
political activities are presided over by the Village Head or Chief, *Eze Ogo*. Usually the *Eze
Ogo* is a direct descendant of the founder of the
village.

Above the village level is the clan government,
which is composed of the Village Heads. The
clan government is presided over by the Clan
Head.

The shrine and work place of a respected diviner, priest, and herbal doctor.

Mbari houses are made as sacrifices to local gods of nature, such as Earth and rivers. A master builder leads the work, creating most of the sculptures, but members of the community help at every stage of construction.

The highest level of the Igbo social structure is the *Nzuko ndi Eze Igbo*, the Igbo Council of Chiefs, which is composed of all the Igbo Clan Heads. When the Federal Government of Nigeria recognized traditional rulers as an important arm of the government, *Nzuko ndi Eze Igbo* began electing a president to represent them at the federal capital, first in Lagos and currently in Abuja.

▼ SUBSTRUCTURES ▼

Below the structures of governance is a web of structures that keeps the Igbo society working harmoniously. They include the roles and positions of ancestors, gods and goddesses, diviners, healers, carvers, hunters, warriors, age-grades, and titled men.

▼ ANCESTORS, GODS, GODDESSES, AND DIVINATION ▼

The Igbo believe that ancestors, gods, and goddesses are part and parcel of their human activities. They believe that when the ancestors or gods and goddesses are offended, sacrifices must be offered to appease them.

Such sacrifices cannot be offered until the will of the ancestors, gods, and goddesses are *divined*, or found out by prophecy. Those who divine the will of the gods and offer sacrifices to them are diviners, priests, and priestesses.

An Igbo carver holds two of his masks dedicated to the god Okoroshi. Carvers believe they are inspired by the gods and goddesses they serve.

Once the diviners have found out the cause of a tragedy or calamity, priests and priestesses offer sacrifices to the gods, and then healers are enabled to heal the sick and the infirm.

Carvers are those who carve masks and images of Igbo gods and goddesses. Like healers and priests, the carvers claim to be inspired by the gods and goddesses they serve. The masks they produce are worn by masquerade dancers during rituals and ceremonies. Also, statues of various gods and goddesses are erected in the shrines and oracles.

▼ THE HUNTER/WARRIOR GROUP ▼

The Igbo communities relied heavily on the hunter/warrior group, made up of people who could hunt wild animals and people with bows and arrows, machetes, spears, and Dane guns. In time, they became traditional warriors, fighting intertribal wars, protecting their homes, farmlands, women, and children from external enemies. Such enemies included neighboring peoples and foreigners who raided their homes for slaves.

Because of their military skill, the hunter/warrior class has become the symbol of Igbo strength, which is celebrated internationally by the "Igbo War Dance."

▼ THE AGE-GRADE SYSTEM ▼

In Igboland, persons born within a period of three years belong to an age-grade. Between the ages of 18 and 21, they are usually named officially by the Village Elders during public ceremonies, which may involve sacrifices and dances to the gods and ancestors, as well as feasting and wrestling.

The majority of the development projects are carried out by various age-grades. An example is Abiriba in Abia State. Abiriba is a model for community development efforts.

▼ THE TITLED GROUP ▼

Because the Igbo regard achievement with

The throne at the left is for a young man who is being elevated to a high title—and high status—at this ceremony.

deep respect, those who have made achievements in their particular occupation like to celebrate them publicly by taking titles. The highest of such traditional titles is celebrated by the *ozo*, which involves the slaughter of many cows for feasting members of the society. Once a man is initiated into it, he goes by the title *Ogbuefi* (killer of cows).

Igbo society has so many titles that the pursuit of them has created great competitiveness in its citizens. Ordinarily, such a situation would create a division between the poor and the rich. But in Igbo society the division is somewhat bridged by the social concept of *onye aghala*

A titled Igbo man and his wife wear elaborate personal decorations on the day of his title-taking ceremony.

nwanneya, "helping one's brother or sister to get up." In other words, the more successful people are, the more they are expected to play the role of their brothers' or sisters' keepers.

▼ THE COMMONWEAL ▼

The Igbo social structure is one that seeks to promote general welfare for all, including spirit beings. Individuals may become very successful or distinguished in their activities or occupations, but their success is measured by how much others benefit from it. Those others are members of one's nuclear family or of the extended family. That is, any Igbo man or woman who can prove any near or remote relationship with another becomes a member of that person's family.

Most Igbo men and women, no matter to which social structure they belong, are eager to obey the laws of the land, *omenala,* and the will of the ancestors and divine beings. They become very traditionally religious. ▲

chapter

4

THE WOMEN'S WORLD

THE IGBO BELIEF IN COMPLEMENTARY dualism makes the women's world as important as the men's; and women fit perfectly in the Igbo social structure that was discussed in Chapter 3. The difference, however, is that men and women are assigned specific roles according to their gender. The very nature of such roles makes men more visible than women to nonmembers of the society.

Women also play most of the roles that men play in all aspects of Igbo life. Whereas men serve as priests of Igbo goddesses, women serve as priestesses of Igbo gods. And the Igbo pantheon has as many goddesses as gods. Also, the most important deity in Igbo traditional religion is the Earth Goddess, Ala.

Woman also play the roles of diviners and healers. In those roles, they frequently serve

as midwives and pediatricians. In addition, some of them are experienced in surgical operations, including circumcision, and treating tropical diseases with herbs.

In Igboland, women belong to the same age-grades as men of their age. When men volunteer to do projects for their villages, women do the same. Sometimes, there is competition between men and women in initiating development projects.

As farmers and traders, men and women are equal partners, but they have different stocks-in-trade, so to speak. Men grow "male" crops like yams, *ji*, whereas women plant "female" ones like cocoyam, *ede*; and while men sell hoes, machetes, and spears, women sell more delicate articles like mats, baskets, and pottery.

In fact, women are not described as "house-wives" in traditional Igbo culture. Some women are known to have given birth to babies on farmlands away from home, only to go back to their work after a resting period of two to three months.

The only occupation from which women are excluded is hunter/warrior service. To the traditional Igbo, women should not be exposed to war. They should rather preserve their bodies and emotions for childbirth and the upbringing of their infants and children.

The training of children is the most impor-

A woman who was selected to help build this *mbari* house finishes painting one of the figures.

Women are wall and body painters in Igboland. Most of their patterns are abstract.

The *ichi* facial scars indicate titled status. Today these scars are found only on older women.

tant work an Igbo man or woman can do for the society. "*Gini ka nnwa*?" (What counts for more than a child?) is a popular saying. If a child is brought up properly, he will grow into a proud and successful Igboman.

Motherhood is so important in traditional Igbo society that men name their daughters *Nneka*, mother-is-supreme. And in some Igbo communities, women who give birth to ten or more children are acknowledged with a ceremony, *igbu ewu ukwu*, the sacrifice of a goat, which some now perform with a cow.

Unfortunately, "barren" women are not

accorded the same respect as the "fruitful" ones. But they may redeem their honor by "marrying" other men (for their husbands' sake), and the children resulting from those marriages become the *bona fide* children of the first marriage.

Igbo women have their own titles. Some are ascribed (come as a result of marrying titled men), and some are acquired. A man who goes by the title of *Nze* ascribes the title of *Lolo* to his wife. However, wealthy women can acquire chieftaincy titles on their own. And some have in the past paid the brideprices of their sons' wives, bought landed properties, and educated their children all by themselves.

In sum, Igbo society is patriarchal, but in many situations power belongs to the women, the first teachers of men and molders of their characters.▲

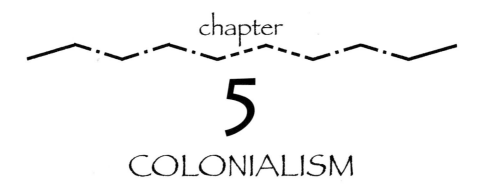

chapter

5

COLONIALISM

THE ACCIDENTAL VISITS THAT THE PORTUGUESE made to the coastal towns of West Africa on their way to India, during the 15th century, exposed African natural and human resources to Europe. Since then, the European world has seen the African continent as a field of exploitation, which began as slave trade and later become colonialism.

Before Nigeria (named after the River Niger in West Africa) became a colony of Great Britain in 1885, it was a territory of several diverse peoples, who were both sovereign and independent of one another. Such peoples had different customs, cultures, governments, economic and educational systems, and languages. In spite of all that, the British imposed on them an alien rule that attempted to bring all the peoples and their cultures under one country and one

government, ruled by Her Majesty, Queen Victoria of England.

In the early period of colonization, the British ran the colony as Northern and Southern Protectorates, and later as Northern and Southern Nigeria. By the late colonial period, Nigeria was divided into three regions: Northern Region (comprising the whole of Northern Nigeria), Western Region, and Eastern Region (both from Southern Nigeria). Finally, in 1964, Mid-Western Region was created out of Southern Nigeria.

In all these creations, however, the British were not so much interested in knowing how such political and administrative arrangements affected the people as they were in achieving administrative convenience. Religion, for example, played a major role in dividing the people rather than uniting them. Northerners were primarily Muslims, whereas Southerners were Christians. And although the British tried hard to promote Western education, the schools were mostly mission schools, whose curricula the British colonial governments could not control. Government had control over the few government secondary schools sited at the federal and regional capital cities: Lagos, Ibadan, Benin, Enugu, and Kaduna. In addition, the Muslims built and ran Islamic institutions, which they preferred to the Western-oriented schools in the south.

These divergent educational and religious institutions had their roots in the precolonial period: in the initial encounter the various regions had had with foreigners during the era of slave trade, and in the way the various peoples had lived before they were grouped into one colony by the British.

As a result of the slave trade, Northern Nigeria came under the control and influence of the Arabs, who not only conquered and enslaved them, but also imposed Islam on them. For their part, the British controlled the coastal towns of Southern Nigeria, including Lagos, Bonny, Opobo, Warri, and Calabar. That is why such places were not only slave centers but also areas that received Christianity and mission education first, before other southern communities like the Igbo, who lived in the hinterland. Nevertheless, when the Scottish explorer Mungo Park explored the Niger, the British moved inland and eventually took over Northern Nigeria from the Arabs.

The late arrival of the British in Igboland was because they could not penetrate the hinterland as easily as they did the coastal towns. And, by the time they attempted to do so, the Igbo merchants had bought and stored Dane guns, Snider guns, and gunpowder for future defense during the era of slave trade. Also, the Igbo were able to produce their own armaments at Igbo-

The British colonists tried to impose their laws and lifestyle on an already well-established people. One example of Igbo culture is shown here. Boys learn the tradition of creating dance masks at a young age by making these colorful costumes from leaves.

Ukwu, Awka, Nkwerre, and Abiriba, which they used to fight the British when they eventually approached. Nevertheless, when the British conquered the Igbo, they did so with the assistance of the Igbo neighbors, who were not happy with Igbo domination.

▼ RESISTANCE OF THE IGBO ▼

Another reason for the prolonged Igbo resistance to British rule is found in their republican attitude. Whereas the Hausa (from the north), the Yoruba (from the west), and the Bini (from the midwest) had kings, the Igbo (from the east) had natural rulers, *Ndi Eze*, who did not wield the kind of authority that the other Nigerian rulers did. In fact, Igbo rulers functioned more or less like heads of families, whose authority was not absolute. That is why the Igbo fought the British with all their might—to avoid the monarchical rule of the British Queen.

Finally, the Igbo, especially Arochukwu merchants, had established many plantations, *unubi*, in southern parts of Nigeria during the era of slave trade. They were not prepared to turn these over to a foreign power; and the Igbo traditional religion—the source of their spiritual, economic, and political prosperity—could not bow to an alien religion. Thus, the Igbo opposition to British rule was the result of their fear of losing their sovereignty and independence, which had distinguished them among their neighbors.

In spite of the battle they gave the British forces, Igboland was eventually colonized. However, the British did not rule directly. Instead, they did so through Igbo Warrant Chiefs and court messengers (*kotma* in Igbo), who were so corrupt and harsh that many preferred to be ruled directly by the British.

As Igbo women saw their husbands and sons who opposed the Warrant Chiefs being sent to jail or shot by the colonial forces, they resolved to take matters into their own hands. They waged guerrilla warfare against the British and won. It was a war that claimed many Igbo women's lives, but it put down the corrupt system that the men could not destroy. In the end, the women were lionized in Nigerian colonial history, which records the event as the Aba Women's Riots, 1929–30. Their role effectively complemented the men's liberation effort and became a model for the Nigerian feminist movement.

▼ IGBO JOIN THE SYSTEM ▼

Once the Igbo came under British rule, they embraced the system fully: Some went to church, many attended the mission schools, and others later went to England and America for higher education.

Although the British rejoiced that they had converted souls and replaced traditional education with their Western system, the Igbo knew that they had to learn the British systems if they were to regroup in the long run to do battle with the British on another field. So they went to school, received higher education, and came back to lead the fight against colonialism and to win independence for their fatherland.

The leader of the politicians who fought and won independence for Nigeria in 1960 was an Igbo, Dr. Nnamdi Azikiwe. He enrolled in the class of 1931 at Lincoln University in the United States, majoring in Political Science. He returned to Nigeria and founded a newspaper, the *West African Pilot*, whose motto was, "Show the light and the people will find their way." A

Some of the Igbo accepted Christianity as their religion.

charismatic leader, he attracted a formidable
following known as the Zikist Movement, which
eventually revived the nationalist political party,
the National Council for Nigeria and the
Cameroons (NCNC). Successively he became the
first Premier of Eastern Region, the first indigenous Governor-General of Nigeria, and the first
President of Nigeria in 1963. Also, he inspired
the establishment of the first indigenous Nigerian
university, The University of Nigeria, Nsukka, in
1960; and he built the first indigenous Nigerian
bank, African Continental Bank (ABC, LTD).

One of the Igbo Zikists, Mazi Mbonu Ojike,

also a graduate of an American institution, was an outstanding nationalist, an eloquent and charming speaker. He advocated the mandatory use of Nigerian dress in public office, instead of the uniforms that the British had introduced. His slogan "Boycott the boycottables" served as a call to Nigerians, who were rapidly becoming "Europeanized," to emphasize their "Africanness."

The list of Igbo leaders during the colonial period is endless, especially between 1945 and 1960, when "the winds of political change" were blowing across the African continent. And that change was inspired by Africans who had been enslaved in Europe, the West Indies, and the Americas. For the Igbo, the inspiration came from Olaudah Equiano, Africanus Horton, and King Ja Ja of Opobo.

Equiano, at the age of eleven, and his sister were kidnapped and sold into slavery in the West Indies. In spite of his slave status, he worked on slave ships. With exceptional courage and determination, he learned to speak, read, and write English, studied mathematics, and took an interest in navigation. In the end, he bought his freedom at the age of 19, traveled to Britain where he worked for the liberation of other African slaves, and took part in arranging to send freed African-American slaves as settlers to Sierra Leone. He settled permanently in

England, where he became a popular platform speaker in the abolitionist cause, and wrote his autobiography, *The Interesting Narrative of the Life of Olaudah Equiano.*

James Africanus Horton, born to Igbo ex-slaves in Sierra Leone in 1835, was enabled to go to secondary school through the generosity of an African West Indian, the colony's Chief Justice. In the end, Horton qualified in medicine at King's College, London, and became an M.D. at Edinburgh. He served as an officer in the British army and worked in different parts of West Africa. Before he died in 1883, he had contributed tremendously toward the betterment of the lives of Africans, establishing a bank in Sierra Leone, and educating another Sierra Leonian Igbo, the poet Christian Cole, to study law in London, according to the author Elizabeth Isichei.

King Ja Ja of Opobo was born Jubo Jubogha in Amaigbo, an Igbo community, and sold into slavery in Bonny. He became a successful businessman, buying his freedom and establishing his own kingdom in Opobo of the Delta state. When the British came to that part of Nigeria, he did battle with them. In the end, he was exiled to the West Indies. That exile gave him the opportunity to help African slaves there to buy their freedom. He was so popular and powerful, even in exile, that when he died in

Although the Igbo eventually accepted some British ways, they fought to retain their own culture and identity. Today, modern urban painters such as "Middle Art" (Augustine Okoye) create works that celebrate Igbo traditions.

1891 his body was repatriated to Nigeria for a royal burial.

▼ A UNIFIED LAND ▼

All Nigerian peoples fought against colonialism. Once they conquered Nigeria, however, the British built a network of roads and bridges that linked all parts of the country, appointed government agencies (including District Commissioners, a regimental army, and police), introduced colonial laws and courts, established schools through missionaries, and, above all, imposed on the people English as a national language for administration, education, business, and trade.

All that was intended to create one nation under the Queen of England and her successors. It was a process that implied ending the ethnic isolation and warfare between the Nigerian peoples. Also, it meant that all Nigerians were able to live and do business in all parts of Nigeria, aware that the British law, as well as its enforcement agencies, would protect them. The Igbo took advantage of the new economic, social, and political situation and went to live in all parts of Nigeria. The British education they received and their own marketing techniques had created new job opportunities for them in the country's civil service, police, armed forces, educational institutions, and companies.

The Igbo worked hard to distinguish themselves in good times and in bad times, in freedom and in bondage, whether in their small families or in their ethnic communities, at home or abroad. Behind that were the driving forces of Igbo solidarity and the undying determination to be free and independent always.▲

6

LIFE AFTER INDEPENDENCE

LIFE AFTER INDEPENDENCE LOOKED VERY hopeful for the Igbo, many of whom had been leaders in the fight against colonialism. The majority of the positions that the British held before independence were now occupied by the Igbo and the Yoruba. However, the Hausa, who had been more influenced by Islamic education than by British education, were at a disadvantage.

▼ CRISIS BEGINS ▼

Three years after independence, however, the quiet optimism that all Nigerian peoples shared died down as a result of the new political, social, and economic problems that beset the young nation. Nigeria was in danger of disintegration.

On the political front, two of the four regions were unstable: The West had bloody political crises; so did the Tiv area (in the North), which

revolted openly against the government. As a result, both regions produced political turmoil that threatened the unity of the entire nation.

Ethnic antagonism and prejudice, which the British had suppressed, resurfaced. It led to general corruption and nepotism at all levels of government and society, including the military, judiciary, police, civil service, and universities.

Furthermore, Western education had stratified and polarized people and bred social and economic warfare between city and village people, the educated and the uneducated, the ruling class (politicians) and the ruled (citizens), and the rich and the poor. Thus, there was general discontent throughout the country.

In the end, a cloud of uncertainty hung over the nation. Nothing seemed to work, in spite of the peaceful demonstrations by students and labor leaders against the regional and federal governments. Finally, on January 15, 1966, the army staged a bloody coup that overthrew the federal government and ushered in a military regime. Many of the coup planners were Igbo.

That same day, assassinations occurred in Kaduna (Hausa area and capital of Northern Region), and at Ibadan (Yoruba area and capital of Western Region). None occurred in Benin (capital of the Mid-West, whose Premier was Igbo), or in Enugu (Igbo area and capital of Eastern Region).

The coup planners handed over the governance of the nation to the highest-ranking Nigerian military officer, Major-General Johnson T.U. Aguiyi-Ironsi, an Igbo. He had been the first African Force Commander of the United Nations Peace-Keeping Operation during the Congo crisis, 1960–63.

▼ A UNITARY GOVERNMENT ▼

During his brief administration, Aguiyi-Ironsi took steps to unite the country by abolishing (through a decree) the regional government system that promoted separatism and mistrust. In its place, he introduced a unitary government that saw the entire country as one territory.

Unfortunately, the Northerners, whose political leaders had been assassinated during the January 15, 1966 coup, misinterpreted his intentions. They feared that the unitary government was a plot by Igbo leaders to dominate the country. In a second military coup lead by northern military officers, Agiuyi-Ironsi and a number of high-ranking Igbo officers were killed.

▼ RETURN TO IGBOLAND ▼

When news spread of the second coup, which took place on July 29, 1966, northern military officers, the police, and armed civilians of the Hausa and Fulani peoples went on a rampage, killing every Igbo they could find in northern

Bustling "motor parks" are just one example of how modernized Igboland has become.

cities such as Kano and Kaduna. This was meant to avenge the deaths of those killed in the January 15 coup. Because the killings were so widespread, then Military Governor of Eastern Nigeria, Colonel Chukwuemeka Odumegwu-Ojukwu, asked all Igbo people living in the North to return to the East. They abandoned their businesses and jobs and returned to their Igbo homeland.

Igbo fear was heightened by the emergence of Colonel Yakubu Gowon, a Hausa, as the new Head of the Federal Military Government and Supreme Commander of the Armed Forces. Gowon reinstated the regional government system that General Aguiyi-Ironsi had abolished in spite of its weakness.

The four regions did not receive equal treatment from the new federal government. Northern Region received more amenities and favoritism than the East, the West, and the Mid-West. Appointments to federal offices and agencies, including the military, were not made on merit. In addition, as a result of the general killings of the Igbo, federal officers could not go to the Igbo communities, nor could Igbo officers and workers visit the federal capital in Lagos. Gowon had sent Hausa and Fulani soldiers to guard federal establishments in all non-Igbo areas.

To restore communications between Eastern Region and the federal government, Military Governor Odumegwu-Ojukwu met Gowon and other top military leaders in January 1967 at Aburi, Ghana. He made some effort to find solutions to the problems between the two sides of the Nigerian conflict. The Aburi Accord was drawn up and signed; but when the delegations returned to their territories, they could not implement it because of their different interpretations of it. So the conflict remained.

▼ BIAFRA ▼

Finally, on May 27, 1967, Odumegwu-Ojukwu was ordered by the Consultative Assembly of Eastern Nigeria to declare the region a sovereign state by the name of Biafra. The meeting was held the same day that Gowon had declared a state of emergency throughout Nigeria. He divided the country into twelve states, giving to Eastern Nigeria three, two of which belonged to the minority groups and the third, East-Central State, belonged to the Igbo people.

Two days later, Odumegwu-Ojukwu declared Eastern Nigeria the sovereign Republic of Biafra. The Biafran Armed Forces promoted him General and Head of the State of Biafra. A month after that, Biafra was blockaded by Nigeria. Gowon, who had also been promoted General, declared war on Biafra. Thus, the Nigeria-Biafra War began. It lasted until January 1970.

While Britain, America, and Russia sided with Nigeria, France initially gave Biafra material help. But it later withdrew its support because of pressure from Britain and America. Biafra approached China for help; but China refused. In the end, Biafra relied on itself.

Biafrans all over the world, including students, contributed money and material to support the war effort. Research and Production (RAP), a group of Biafran scientists, scholars, and members of the Army Corps of Engineers, produced a powerful land mine, *ogbunigwe*, rockets, and other armaments, and also refined crude oil for military and domestic use.

Each Biafran community formed a land army

that produced food for the citizens. Civil Defense Committees ensured that each community was defended against enemies within, while soldiers defended Biafra against enemies without.

As the war dragged on, some non-Igbo communities in Biafra defected to the Nigerian side. Nigeria declared to the world that the Biafran cause was an Igbo affair. But non-Igbo Biafran officers like General Effiong and Professor Eyo Ita remained loyal to the cause throughout.

By the end of 1969, the war had claimed more than 1.5 million Igbo lives. Children were dying from malnutrition, which produced such deadly diseases as kwashiorkor and marasmus, and there was general sabotage and corruption within the rank and file of the Biafran armed forces. Without further supply of arms, and having been totally cut off from the rest of the world by the Nigerian blockade, Biafra could not go on. So, on January 15, 1970, Biafra surrendered unconditionally to Nigeria and became part of Nigeria once again.

In accepting the documents of surrender from the Biafran delegation, the Nigerian Head of State, General Gowon, declared that "there were no victors and no vanquished." He had declared publicly that the war was fought to keep Nigeria one. He granted all Biafrans general amnesty.

However, to the general public, which was

The father of this family is the priest of his family's medicine shrine. This is only one of many enduring traits of traditional Igbo culture.

less philosophical about the end of the war, Biafra was defeated and Nigeria was victorious. Nigerian troops raped Biafran women and children and shot some prominent Igbo leaders, including Professor Kalu Ezera, the Vice Chancellor of the University of Biafra. The first indigenous Nigerian university, the University of Nigeria, Nsukka (in Igboland), was burned down. Many Biafran troops committed suicide as a result of the defeat.

In spite of all that, though, the Biafrans earned the respect of Nigeria and the outside world. In addition, Biafran technological ingenu-

ity became vital to the technological culture of postwar Nigeria.

The significance of Biafra was perhaps best described by the Biafran leader himself, General Odumegwu-Ojukwu, who wrote:

> The Biafrans sought to demonstrate once and for all the innate ability of a black people to establish true independence within a polity. The proclamation of the Biafran Republic was at best the delimitation of the people's last defensive position (our last ditch). . .
>
> The philosophy that gave birth to Biafra was that of self-defense. It was not one of abandonment, neither was it one of separation. It was an attempt to found a base, an alternative base from which to continue our combat against neocolonialism in Africa.
>
> Winning or losing a war depends very much on the war aims of the combatants. For Nigeria, that aim was to reintegrate Biafra willy-nilly into the Nigerian polity. Today, we are proud members of the Nigerian polity, hence the internationally achieved victory of Nigeria. For Biafra, the aim of the war was to survive, nothing more, nothing less. Today, we not only have survived but have guaranteed that survival in Nigeria by establishing an identity which is internationally recognized. To that extent the Biafrans were victorious.

It is this fact that made the "no victor no vanquished" postwar policy not only possible but mandatory (*Because I Am Involved*).

For the Igbo, life after independence began with much hope because of the leadership role they had played in the fight against colonialism. Despite the hardship that followed, today the Igbo people live in postwar Nigeria as proud as ever before.▲

chapter

7

POLITICAL AND
SOCIAL CHANGES

WITH THE NIGERIA-BIAFRA WAR OVER, THE
Igbo accepted wholeheartedly the realities of
their new social and political lives in Nigeria.
They had to accept the twelve-state structure of
government that General Gowon had imposed
on the nation by decree. That acceptance was a
part of their survival. The Igbo went to work
immediately to make their home state, East-
Central State, one of the best in the country.

School children were taught under shed trees;
traders revived the ancient commercial tradition
of trade by barter, and others, including university professors, took up odd jobs to ensure that
they survived that difficult phase of their lives.

Those who had relatives abroad called on
them for financial and material assistance. Busi-
nessmen and other professionals who had bank
accounts outside of Biafra withdrew large

amounts of money for the reconstruction of their homes and communities. Above all, some trustworthy Hausa friends and neighbors of the Igbo, who had collected rent on properties vacated by the Igbo, sent what they had collected to the Igbo after the war. It was a gesture that began the postwar friendship between the two prewar enemies. Thus, paradoxically, the war removed much of the bitterness of separatism that, among other factors, had caused the war in the first place. Not all postwar developments were as promising. For instance, southern Igbo neighbors, such as the Delta peoples, had seized Igbo properties, which they branded as "abandoned properties."

Socially, the war brought out the best and the worst of all Nigerians. For the first time, the Igbo and the Hausa realized the humanity in each other. Conversely, the Igbo experienced a strong split with their southern neighbors. The Igbo began to accept Islam as a viable religion, and so permitted the Hausa and Fulani religious leaders to build the first mosques in Igboland. Also, for the first time, Hausa and Fulani men were encouraged to marry Igbo women in great numbers.

The social trust that had been created between the Igbo and the Hausa and Fulani peoples encouraged a new political alliance, which continued in subsequent military regimes. For example, in 1984, when General Ibrahim

Roadside vegetable markets are common sights on roads off the busy highways in Nigeria.

The Igbo have managed to reconcile their traditional culture with Western culture. Billboard advertisements, such as this one for a barber shop, have become a popular art form in Igboland and in many parts of West Africa.

Babangida, a Hausa, became Head of State, he appointed Commodore Ebitu Ukiwe, an Igbo, Chief of General Staff. He also appointed Major-General Ike Nwachukwu, an Igbo, as Foreign Minister.

Economically, ordinary Igbo men and women have created commercial alliances with the Hausa. Even though the Igbo do not live in Hausaland in great numbers as they did before the war, they have formed such strong business partnerships with the Hausa that they have reclaimed many of their "abandoned properties" and opened new and profitable businesses. So, today, some of the Igbo states, especially Abia and Imo, are among the more progressive and prosperous states in Nigeria.▲

At the towering height of 16 feet and 7 feet in diameter, Igbo *Ijele* masks are the largest masks in West Africa.

Conclusion

ON THE SURFACE, THE POLITICAL AND SOCIAL changes that have taken place in postwar Igboland have brought greater prosperity and political participation. Considering how quickly war-torn Igboland was rebuilt, it is as if the war never took place. And the war is almost never mentioned in conversation: no heroes and no saboteurs. Yet the realistic situation is that some victims of the war are still unrecognized by Nigeria as needing national help: Beggars flood the streets of some Igbo communities, many people committed suicide at the end of the war, leaving behind them orphans and widows, some youths permanently lost the chance to receive good education, and others live as permanent amputees. But the worst changes that took place in Igbo social and political life are psychic: The nationalism, morality, and spirituality of the tra-ditional Igbo were shaken. As the Igbo embark on cultural revival, they will undoubtedly continue to take measures to recover those virtues that made them truly great before the war.▲

Glossary

affiliation Close association or connection as in political association.

Ala The Earth Goddess.

ala mmo Spirit world.

ama Village.

amnesty General pardon for offenses, especially political offenses.

Chukwu Igbo high god.

colonialism System or policy by which a nation seeks to extend or retain its authority over other peoples or territories.

elu igwe The sky.

elu uwa The earth.

ethnography The branch of anthropology dealing with the scientific description of individual cultures.

Eze ezi Compound Head.

Eze ogo Village head.

ezi Bloc or section of a village.

kwashiorkor Severe malnutrition caused by a diet low in protein.

Lolo A titled woman.

mba Town or clan, or the people who inhabit it.

libation Form of sacrifice to a deity.

marasmus   State of chronic malnutrition caused by a diet lacking in calories and proteins.

monarchy   Government in which the supreme power is lodged in a monarch.

nationalism   Devotion and loyalty to one's own nation; patriotism.

nsibiri   A secret Igbo language system like the Egyptian hieroglyphics.

nso Ala   An abomination or crime against the Earth Goddess.

nwanyi   Female; woman.

nwoke   Male; man.

Nze   Titled man.

obi   Household or ancestral home of the agnate family.

obodo   Village or town.

Ogbuefi   Titleholder, especially of the *ozo* title.

omenala   Custom.

ozo   Titled group.

pan-   Prefix meaning "all," as in pan-Igbo.

umunna   Family in which kinship is based on a male.

unubi   Plantation.

For Further Reading

Achebe, Chinua. *The Trouble with Nigeria.* Enugu, Nigeria: Fourth Dimension Publishing Company Ltd., 1983.

Afigbo, Adiele. *Ropes of Sand: Studies in Igbo History and Culture.* Ibadan, Nigeria: University Press Ltd., 1981.

Equiano, Olaudah. *The Interesting Narrative of the Life of Olaudah Equiano.* Portsmouth, NH: Heinemann, 1969.

Isichei, Elizabeth. *A History of the Igbo People.* London: The Macmillan Press Ltd., 1976.

Odumegwu-Ojukwu, Emeka. *Because I Am Involved.* Ibadan, Nigeria: Spectrum Books Ltd., 1989.

Ogbaa, Kalu. *Gods, Oracles, and Divination: Folkways in Chinua Achebe's Novels.* Trenton, NJ: Africa World Press, 1992.

Ojike, Mazi Mbonu, *My Africa.* New York: The John Day Company, 1946.

Uchendu, Victor C. *The Igbo of Southeast Nigeria.* New York: Holt, Rinehart and Winston, 1965.

Index

ABOUT THE AUTHOR

Kalu Ogbaa was born and reared in Umuchiakuma Ihechiowa in Arochukwu Local Government Area, an Igbo community, in Nigeria.

He is currently Associate Professor of English at Southern Connecticut State University, New Haven, where he teaches African-American, African, and Commonwealth literatures.

He received a B.A. (Hons) degree from the University of Nigeria, Nsukka; an M.A. from Ohio State University, Columbus; and a Ph.D. from the University of Texas at Austin. He is a member of the Distinguished Scholars Honor Society of *Phi Kappa Phi*, USA, and Fellow of the International Biographical Association, Cambridge, England.

Professor Ogbaa is the author of *Gods, Oracles, and Divination: Folkways in Chinua Achebe's Novels* (1992), *The Gong and the Flute: African Literary Development and Celebration* (1994), and numerous articles on Black and Commonwealth literatures.

PHOTO CREDITS: Herbert M. Cole
DESIGN: Kim Sonsky